J. William Zoldak

Grandpa's Bumble Bee Story

Illustrations by Misti Feliciano Hobbs

Grandpa's Bumble Bee Story
J. William Zoldak

FIRST EDITION

Hardcover ISBN: 9781088051320
Softcover ISBN: 9781088051054

ALL RIGHTS RESERVED.

©2022 J. William Zoldak
Illustrations by Misti Feliciano Hobbs.

No part of this publication may be translated, reproduced or transmitted in any form without prior permission in writing from the publisher.

STONEHEDGES

Published by Stonehedges
OXFORD, MASSACHUSETTS

Dear Grandchildren,

I've always been fascinated with bees, especially bumble bees. When I was young, I watched them as they moved from flower to flower with what seemed like effortless motion, and then they would fly off to some distant place. As I got older, I learned the different kinds of bees and their importance to the environment. I learned that while collecting pollen for their own use, they pollinated the plants as they moved from one flower to the next. The end result was the production of fruit and seeds. It's all part of one amazing continuous cycle.

I often think of bumble bees as the gentle giants of the bee world. They appear larger than other bees and they, like their cousins the honey bees, are less aggressive than some of their other relatives. Bumble bees will, however, sting if they are provoked. I remember once when I was very young, I tried to pet a bumble because it seemed cute and fuzzy to me. It stung me immediately teaching me a lesson that I never forgot. I never did that again.

While honey bees are best known for producing the honey that we buy in the stores, bumble bees also produce honey but on a far smaller scale. Today, of course, all bees are being threatened by pesticides and other environmental problems so I thought it might be helpful and important to tell you about these amazing little creatures. Hopefully, this story will help you appreciate the bee world and your place in it.

The Humble Bumble Bees

While strolling through some fields of brush,

I saw a gentle giant on the rush.

I followed it to its humble home,

To discover that it lived not alone.

Well hidden behind a bush I saw,
The narrow opening to its front hall.
It appeared to lead into the ground,
Where I could hear a muffled buzzing sound.

It saw me not I am sure of that,
So, there I waited, so there I sat.
It wasn't long before I could see,
The place was filled with activity.

The furry giants would go and roam,
Returning later to their humble home.
They worked right through the midday heat,
Carrying pollen gold upon their feet.

Far, far from home their paths would lead,

In search of flower plants and common weed.

Trip after trip too many to count,

From dawn to dusk their miles would mount.

I came to watch them most every day,
As they worked on with no time to play.
Through the summer their numbers increased.
Fondness grew within me for these beasts.

As warm summer days began to fall,
These gentle giants met natures call.
They began to disappear one by one,
And to my regret, soon there were none.

Then through the dark dreary winter storms,
As I walked the brush and meadow thorns,
My thoughts wandered to those golden days,
To the place where the gentle giant stays.

When the winter broke and the spring had come,

I anxiously watched the meadow run,

And one day as I passed the bush of old,

I heard beneath it a sound unfold.

It wasn't long before I could see,

The place had some small activity.

A gentle giant, yellow and black,

Came from the ground a little crack.

It flew on to a meadow flower,
And there it gathered pollen power.
Then as the Spring days passed on by,
More lovely creatures began to fly.

Well, now it's midsummer as before,
And I am watching the same front door.
The gentle giants come and go, as they please,
For they are the lovely, humble, bumble bees.

Now as I close this letter, I would like to leave you with a few thoughts about these beautiful creatures of yellow and black. First, in case you might have missed it, this story/poem is about the life cycle of bumble bees. It takes you through the seasons of the year and the activity of these bees as time passes. Notice the location of their nests and how their numbers rise and fall as the seasons pass. Remember we must do all we can to protect them and their environment. For their lives may depend on it and ours as well.

With love as always,

Grandpa.

The Buzz on Bumbles Bees

(Life Cycle)

- The queen bee comes out of hibernation in the early spring.
- She has spent the entire winter underground.
- The fat stored in her body has provided her with nourishment through the winter.
- After hibernation, she gets nourishment from nearby flower pollen.
- She then selects a nest site.
- Nest sites are usually a hole in the ground, a rock wall, or other protected structures.
- The queen prepares a place within the nest to lay the eggs and store food.
- Soon after tiny larvae are hatched from the eggs.
- The larvae are fed by pollen that the queen obtains from nearby flowers.
- As the larvae grow, they form a cocoon.
- Not long afterwards, the cocoons open, and new bees are born.

- The first batch of bees are all female worker bees.
- These worker bees collect pollen to feed the hive/nest.
- They also clean and guard the nest from intruders.
- The queen continues producing more batches of bees throughout the summer.
- The colony may grow to as large as several hundred bees.
- The last batch of bees born in the fall are all young queens and males (no workers).
- These young queens' and males leave the nest never to return.
- The young queens mate with male bees from other nests (not from their own).
- After mating, the males die.
- As this is happening, the bee population in the colony is decreasing also.
- Finally, all the bees die (including the old queen), leaving only the young queens.
- As winter approaches, the young queens feed heavily from the flowers.
- The fat stored in their bodies prepares them for hibernation.
- These queens, now fattened, burrow into the ground, remaining there through the winter.
- In the Spring the queen bees come out of hibernation to start the cycle again.

More Bumble Facts

- Each bumble bee nest has only one queen and she produces all of the offspring.

- There are about 250 species of bumble bees (most people can't tell them apart).

- Experts say that, aerodynamically, bumbles shouldn't be able to fly. No one told them.

- Bumble bees wings beat over 130 times a second.

- Bumble bees don't die after they sting like some other bees do.

www.ingramcontent.com/pod-product-compliance
Lightning Source LLC
Chambersburg PA
CBHW061149010526
44118CB00026B/2920